My First Book About Beavers

Amazing Animal Books
Children's Picture Books

By Molly Davidson

Mendon Cottage Books

JD-Biz Publishing

Read More Amazing Animal Books

Table of Contents

Facts About Beavers

Beavers are more active at night.

They do not have very good eye sight, but they can smell and hear extra well.

Beavers live both on land and in the water.

The babies of a beaver are called a "kit."

The national animal of Canada is the beaver.

Beavers can hold their breath underwater for more than 15 minutes.

Beavers slap their tails on the water to warn others of danger.

Beavers are part of the rodent family.

Beavers' teeth keep growing their whole lives.

They need their teeth to cut down trees to build dams.

Beavers live about 12 - 15 years, but some live to be 20 years old.

Beavers

Beavers are most known for the dams they build in lakes, rivers, and streams.

Beavers like to build dams so they create a pool of water, for safety, for themselves and family.

Beavers build lodges with all the trees they cut down.

The entrance to these lodges is usually underwater; this also helps protect the beavers.

Beavers have oily fur which covers their body, it makes them waterproof.

Beavers swim at a speed of about 5 miles per hour (mph).

Beaver Tails

A beaver's tail is long and flat, it is usually 1 1/2 feet long by 1 foot wide, and it has no fur on it.

Beavers use their tail for balance when chewing down trees.

Beaver Tail

They will use their tails for steering while swimming.

A beaver's tail helps keep them cool, since it does not have fur, heat can be released.

Beaver tails are made of the same skin that human noses are made of.

Muskrat

Sometimes people think muskrats are beaver but a muskrat is smaller and has a round tail.

Beaver Dams

A beaver dam is a mix of trees that have been chewed down and stacked by the beavers.

All the holes will be filled with weeds and mud.

The dam will stop water from going its normal way; this will create a pond around the dam, to keep the beavers safe.

Beavers will cut down extra trees to be stored for around, so they can eat the leaves later on, without leaving their home.

Beavers Habitat

Beavers live on land and in the water, mostly in the water.

Beaver eating a grass by a lake in Yellowstone

Beavers have clear eyelids, which act like goggles, when they are swimming.

Beavers need to live where there is water and lots of trees for them to cut down.

Beavers live in lodges that they build, which is usually in the middle of a pond that they created.

Sometimes beavers will dig deep into the side of a river bank; here they will store food to be eaten in the winter.

Beaver Houses

If a beaver colony (group) is large they will build more than one dam to help protect them.

Beaver lodge in early Spring

Beavers' houses are called a lodge.

Lodges can be 10 - 20 feet long and 8 feet tall, above the water.

In one week Beavers can build dams as long as 1,000 feet!

If one destroys a beaver dam without killing the beaver, it will do no good, the beaver will have it rebuild or repaired in just a few days.

Beavers have up to 5 underwater entrances to their lodges. It makes it almost impossible for other animals to get in.

What Beavers Eat

Beavers eat mostly water plants like water lilies, cattails, sedges, their favorites are clover and raspberry canes.

Beavers also enjoy eating leaves off trees and sometimes the bark, roots, and branches of the trees.

Beavers do not eat fish or other water animals, just plants.

These rodents do not hibernate; they pile their food storage for winter.

They store sticks underwater and survive on these sticks when the pond freezes.

They live underwater for the whole winter and nibble on the sticks that they have stored.

Trapping Beavers

For almost 300 years fur trapping was a major industry in the U.S. and Canada.

Fur trappers helped map out the countries since they were traveling across it.

They would sell the fur, called a pelt, to people in Europe; they would make hats and scarves with them.

These fur trappers, also called mountain men, made friends with the Native Americans.

The Native Americans could trade their pelts for guns, knives, beads, and other items they couldn't make themselves.

Not much fur trapping goes on now. The main reason people trap beavers, is to stop them from damaging their land.

This trapping is many times done in a no-kill trap, so the land owners just move the beavers to somewhere else, where they can be happy.

Horses For Kids
Amazing Animal Books For Young Readers
By John and Annalee Davidson

Ponies For Kids
Mendon Cottage Books
AmazingAnimalBooks For Young Readers
Rachel Smith

Ten Amazing Horses For Kids
Nature Books for Kids
JD-Biz Publishing
K. Bennett

Akhal-Teke "The Golden Horse Of the desert" For Kids
Nature Books for Kids
JD-Biz Publishing
K. Bennett

Suffolk-Punch "The Gentle Giant" For Kids
Nature Books for Kids
JD-Biz Publishing
K. Bennett

Shires "The great Horse" For Kids
Nature Books for Kids
JD-Biz Publishing
K. Bennett

Colonial Spanish "Horse of the Americas" For Kids
Nature Books for Kids
JD-Biz Publishing
K. Bennett

Canadian "The Little Iron Horse" For Kids
Nature Books for Kids
JD-Biz Publishing
K. Bennett

Cleveland Bays "History and Future" Horses For Kids
Nature Books for Kids
JD-Biz Publishing
K. Bennett

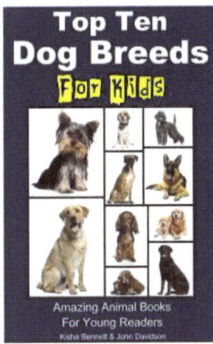

Top Ten Dog Breeds For Kids

Amazing Animal Books For Young Readers
Kisha Bennett & John Davidson

German Shepherds

Dog Books for Kids
K. Bennett

Bulldogs

Dog Books for Kids
K. Bennett

Dachshund

Dog Books for Kids
K. Bennett

Poodles

Dog Books for Kids
K. Bennett

Labrador Retrievers

Dog Books for Kids
K. Bennett

Rottweilers

Dog Books for Kids
K. Bennett

Boxers

Dog Books for Kids
K. Bennett

Golden Retrievers

Dog Books for Kids
K. Bennett

Puppies

Dog Books For Kids

Amazing Animal Books
By John Davidson

Beagles

Dog Books for Kids
K. Bennett

Yorkshire Terriers

Dog Books for Kids
K. Bennett

**Dogs
Top Ten Dog Breeds For Kids**

Amazing Animal Books
For Young Readers
Zahra Jazeel & John Davidson

Cats For Kids

Amazing Animal Books
For Young Readers
K. Bennett & John Davidson

Foxes For Kids

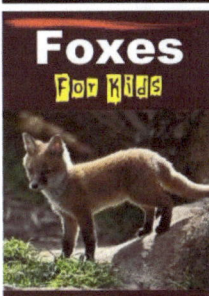

Amazing Animal Books
For Young Readers
Zahra Jazeel & John Davidson

Wolves For Kids

Amazing Animal Books
For Young Readers
By John Davidson and Virginia Fidler

Publisher

JD-Biz Corp

P O Box 374

Mendon, Utah 84325

http://www.jd-biz.com/

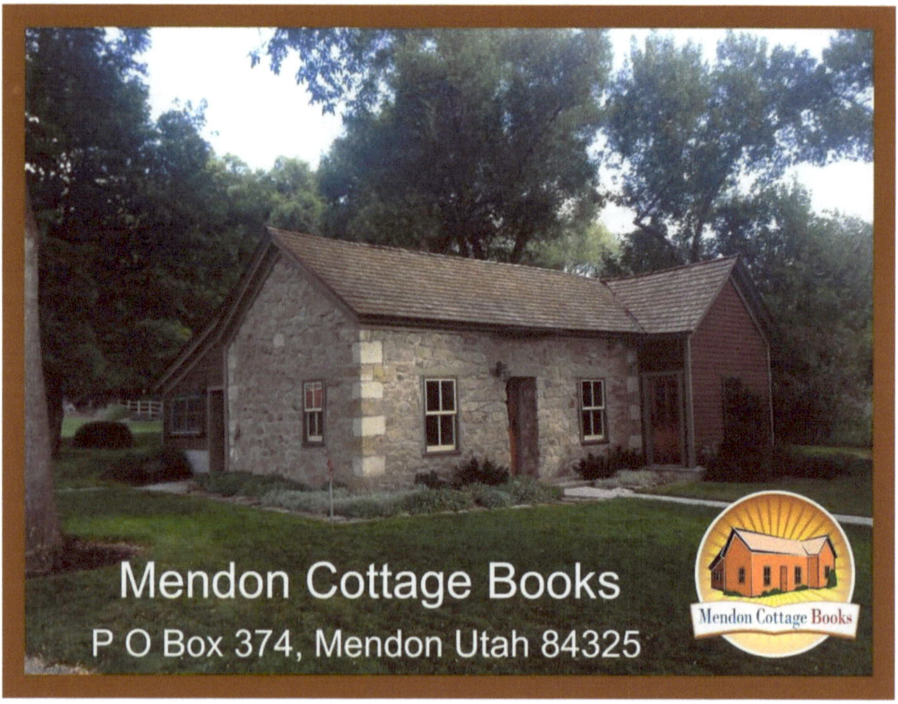

Mendon Cottage Books

P O Box 374, Mendon Utah 84325

www.ingramcontent.com/pod-product-compliance
Lightning Source LLC
Chambersburg PA
CBHW050924290526
45792CB00002B/879